AMERICAN CITIZENSHIP

MODERN
POLITICAL PARTIES

by Lydia Bjornlund

Content Consultant
Richard Bell
Associate Professor, Department of History
University of Maryland

Core Library

An Imprint of Abdo Publishing
abdopublishing.com

abdopublishing.com

Published by Abdo Publishing, a division of ABDO, PO Box 398166, Minneapolis, Minnesota 55439. Copyright © 2017 by Abdo Consulting Group, Inc. International copyrights reserved in all countries. No part of this book may be reproduced in any form without written permission from the publisher. Core Library™ is a trademark and logo of Abdo Publishing.

Printed in the United States of America, North Mankato, Minnesota
042016
092016

THIS BOOK CONTAINS
RECYCLED MATERIALS

Cover Photo: Ron Sachs/picture-alliance/dpa/AP Images
Interior Photos: Ron Sachs/picture-alliance/dpa/AP Images, 1; Steve Helber/AP Images, 4; Red Line Editorial, 7, 26; Daniel Acker/Bloomberg/Getty Images, 9; Ethan Miller/Getty Images, 12; Library of Congress, 15; White House, 16; USNWR/Alamy, 20; John Bazemore/AP Images, 25; Jim Watson/AFP/Getty Images, 28, 45; Robert Nickelsberg/Getty Images, 31; J. Scott Applewhite/AP Images, 33; Brian Kersey/Getty Images, 34, 43; Ann Heisenfelt/AP Images, 36; Olivier Douliery/Getty Images, 39; Luke Sharrett/Bloomberg/Getty Images, 41

Editor: Sharon Doorasamy
Series Designer: Laura Polzin

Cataloging-in-Publication Data
Names: Bjornlund, Lydia, author.
Title: Modern political parties / by Lydia Bjornlund.
Description: Minneapolis, MN : Abdo Publishing, [2017] | Series: American
    citizenship | Includes bibliographical references and index.
Identifiers: LCCN 2015960483 | ISBN 9781680782424 (lib. bdg.) |
    ISBN 9781680776539 (ebook)
Subjects: LCSH: Political parties--United States--Juvenile literature. | Political
    campaigns--United States--Juvenile literature. | United States--Politics and
    government--Juvenile literature.
Classification: DDC 324--dc23
LC record available at http://lccn.loc.gov/2015960483

CONTENTS

CHAPTER ONE

THE RISE OF POLITICAL PARTIES

Political parties serve an important role in American society. People in these organizations share common values and beliefs. Parties pick political candidates. They help voters make choices. It may be hard to research every candidate's positions. Political parties can give voters a general sense of what candidates believe.

Modern political parties help voters make choices about candidates standing for election.

The First Political Parties

The US Constitution does not mention political parties. The document's writers distrusted parties. When they wrote the Constitution, the United States had just won its freedom from Britain. Independence came after the American Revolution (1775–1783). Some leaders worried disagreements might cause the new government to crumble. President George Washington advised against forming "factions," or parties.

Parties arose because people had differing ideas. Alexander Hamilton believed in a strong national government. In 1787 his followers began calling themselves

Federalists	Democratic-Republicans
Founded circa 1791–1794; dissolved 1824	Founded circa 1791–1798; dissolved 1825
Led by Alexander Hamilton	Led by Thomas Jefferson
Favored strong federal government	Favored power remaining with the states
Focused on manufacturing and commerce	Focused on planters and farmers
Support centered in New England states	Support centered in South and West

The First Political Parties

This chart shows the differences between the first two political parties in the United States. What can you tell about the parties' regions based on the parties' political beliefs?

the Federalists. The Federalists became the first US political party.

Thomas Jefferson disagreed with Hamilton. He wanted local and state governments to hold most of the power. Jefferson and James Madison formed a party to oppose the Federalists. This party became known as the Democratic-Republicans.

John Adams ran as a Federalist Party candidate for president in 1796. He ran against Jefferson. Adams won. Jefferson won the next presidential election in 1800. This marked the first peaceful exchange of power between two parties.

US Political Parties Today

These two parties have since died out. Many others have risen in their places. For most of US history there have been two main parties. Today they are the Republican Party and the Democratic Party.

Smaller parties are called third parties. One of the largest is the Green Party. It focuses on environmental issues. The Libertarian Party is another third party. It focuses on individual rights and less government control.

Factions sometimes form within parties. The Tea Party is a faction within the Republican Party. Since

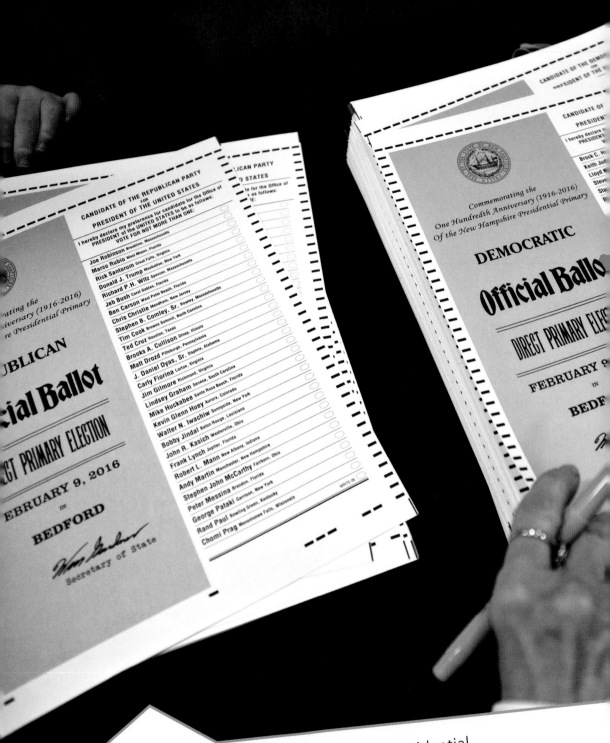

Ballots for Democratic and Republican presidential candidates sit on a sign-in table in New Hampshire on February 9, 2016.

it formed in 2009, the Tea Party has gained many followers.

Today's parties are large organizations. They select candidates to run for offices ranging from mayor to the president of the United States. They choose what policies the government will consider. They have become an important part of politics.

What Is Politics?

Politics is sometimes defined as the science or practice of holding public office or taking part in government. A central element of politics is winning elections. Political parties work hard to get their candidates elected to public office.

George Washington left the presidency after eight years. He gave advice to citizens and their leaders in his farewell address:

> *The alternate domination of one faction over another, sharpened by the spirit of revenge, natural to party [disagreement], which in different ages and countries has perpetrated the most horrid enormities, is itself a frightful despotism. . . . There is an opinion that parties in free countries are useful checks upon the administration of the Government, and serve to keep alive the spirit of Liberty. This within certain limits is probably true . . . [but] in Governments purely elective, it is a spirit not to be encouraged.*

Source: "Washington's Farewell Address." The Papers of George Washington. University of Virginia, n.d. Web. Accessed March 14, 2016.

Changing Minds

This passage discusses George Washington's view of factions. Do you agree or disagree with Washington? Imagine you are writing to a friend. Explain why you either support or disapprove of political parties. What reasons would you give? Use facts and details to support your reasons.

CHAPTER TWO

THE TWO-PARTY SYSTEM

The Republican and Democratic parties dominate US politics today. More than 72 million Americans belong to the Democratic Party. Approximately 55 million Americans are Republican Party members.

The Democratic Party formed in 1828. Andrew Jackson was elected president that year. Several factions had supported Jackson's election. Jackson

Supporters of Democratic presidential candidate Hillary Clinton cheer in Las Vegas, Nevada, on February 20, 2016.

The Electoral College

The US president is not elected directly by voters. The Electoral College decides who will be president. Each state chooses representatives called electors. The number of electors is equal to the state's total number of senators and representatives. A candidate must win more than half of all the electors' votes to become president.

A presidential candidate can win the national popular vote yet lose the presidency. This has happened four times in US history, most recently in 2000. More people voted for Democratic candidate Al Gore. But Republican George W. Bush won more votes in the Electoral College. Bush became president.

united them into the Democratic Party. The Republican Party began in 1854. It is also known as the Grand Old Party (GOP). Abraham Lincoln was elected the first Republican president in 1860.

The two parties outline their beliefs in platforms. Platforms spell out positions on important issues. Parties write their platforms at conventions. These conventions take place before presidential elections. These elections are held every four years.

Abraham Lincoln served as president until his assassination in April 1865.

Republican president George W. Bush was elected in 2000 and served until President Barack Obama took office in 2009.

Party platforms sometimes change over time.

The Republican Party Platform

In 2016 the Republican Party platform supported smaller government. It also favored lower taxes. Republicans tend to believe many government rules are unnecessary.

The Republican Party generally opposes abortion and same-sex marriage. It tends to support increases in military spending. The party also believes the United States should play a leading role in international affairs.

Political Party Symbols

The elephant is the Republican Party's symbol. The Democratic Party's is the donkey. Both symbols started out as insults. Andrew Jackson ran for president in 1828. His opponents compared him to a stubborn donkey. Jackson turned the insult to his favor. He put the donkey on campaign posters. Cartoonist Thomas Nast made the donkey famous. He began using it in newspaper cartoons. In 1874 Nast showed a donkey dressed in lion's skin scaring an elephant. The elephant became the Republican Party's symbol.

The Democratic Party Platform

Democrats support US involvement in world politics. But the Democratic Party does not generally support increasing military spending. The Democratic Party also supports aid for poor countries.

The Democratic Party platform ranks environmental protection as a high priority. The party typically supports abortion rights, same-sex marriage, and welfare for poor Americans. Democrats tend to advocate higher taxes for wealthy Americans and businesses.

Coming Together

Political parties propose platforms so that Americans know where the parties stand and can make informed voting choices. Republicans and Democrats must work together after elections. The two parties come together to help the citizens they represent in federal, state, and local governments.

Abraham Lincoln was the first presidential nominee of the Republican Party. He expressed his views on the role of government in notes dated July 1, 1854:

> The legitimate object of government is to do for a community of people whatever they need to have done, but cannot do at all, or cannot so well do, for themselves, in their separate and individual capacities. In all that the people can individually do as well for themselves, government ought not to interfere. The desirable things which the individuals of a people cannot do, or cannot well do, for themselves, fall into two classes: those which have relations to wrongs, and those which have not. . . . The first—that in relation to wrongs—embraces all crimes [and breaking the law.] The other embraces all which, in its nature, and without wrong, requires combined action, as public roads and highways, public schools, charities . . . and the machinery of government itself.

Source: Abraham Lincoln. "The Object of Government." Civil War Trust. *The Civil War Trust*, n.d. Web. Accessed January 28, 2016.

What's the Big Idea?

Take a close look at this passage. What is the main idea? How did Lincoln feel about government? Explain your answer.

CHAPTER THREE

THIRD PARTIES

Many Americans are dissatisfied with the Republican and Democratic parties. They support third-party candidates. Americans have formed new parties throughout the country's history.

Theodore Roosevelt failed to win the Republican Party's nomination for president in 1912. He formed the Progressive Party. In 1968 the Democrats did not

Theodore Roosevelt was one of the most successful third-party presidential candidates in US history.

nominate George Wallace. He ran as the candidate of the American Independent Party instead.

Today more than 50 US political parties exist. The Libertarian Party is one of the largest. It has approximately 330,000 members. The party emphasizes individual freedoms. It also believes in limited government. The Green Party formed in 1984. It is focused on the environment. The Constitution Party began in 1991 as the US Taxpayers' Party. It changed its name in 2000. The party believes in a strict reading of the US Constitution.

Barriers to Third Parties

Third parties face many obstacles to winning presidential elections. The names of Democratic and Republican candidates are automatically added to ballots, the papers on which voters enter their choices. Third-party candidates must get thousands of signatures to be added. It is also difficult for these candidates to appear in televised debates.

Another barrier is the US electoral system. Nearly all US elections follow the winner-take-all approach. This means that whoever gets the most votes wins. But there are several types of voting systems. Most other Western democracies have proportional systems instead. Voters mark on their ballots which party they prefer. The party then gets seats in proportion to its share of the total popular vote. A party that gets 25 percent of the votes gets 25 percent of the seats in the legislature.

The Influence of Third Parties

Third-party candidates are more successful in state and local elections. Libertarian candidates often win in western states. So do Green Party candidates. Socialist

Proportional Representation

About 90 democratic nations use proportional representation. Four political parties currently represent voters in Germany's congress. Russia, Spain, and Brazil also have proportional representation. Israel currently has ten parties. Forty-five countries use winner-take-all systems.

candidates have won in the northeast. Vermont senator Bernie Sanders won as an independent in 2012. Sanders then ran for president in 2016 as a Democrat.

Some third-party candidates run knowing they are unlikely to win. But they run anyway. They run to bring attention to an important issue. Or they run to promote a new idea. Mainstream candidates may adopt the ideas if they become popular. They may even become a part of a major party's platform. This happened in 1992. The Reform Party nominated Ross Perot for president. Perot ran to reduce the federal deficit. A deficit occurs when

Presidential hopeful Senator Bernie Sanders speaks during a rally on February 21, 2016, in Greenville, South Carolina.

Year	Party	Candidate	Percentage of Popular Vote	Number of Electoral Votes
1912	Progressive	Theodore Roosevelt	27.5	88
1912	Socialist	Eugene V. Debs	6.0	0
1924	Progressive	Robert M. La Follette	16.6	13
1948	States' Rights	Strom Thurmond	2.4	39
1980	American Independent	George Wallace	13.5	46
1980	Independent	John Anderson	6.6	0
1992	Reform	H. Ross Perot	18.9	0
1996	Reform	H. Ross Perot	8.4	0
2000	Green	Ralph Nader	2.7	0

Notable Third-Party Candidates

No third-party candidate has ever won the presidency. Some candidates have made impressive showings, though. This list shows some of the candidates who have won 1 percent or more of the vote. The parties they represented are also listed. What can you conclude about the influence of third parties based on this chart?

the government spends more money than it takes in. Other parties had not chosen this problem as a campaign issue. Perot won 18.9 percent of the popular vote. Since 1992 reducing the federal deficit has been an election issue.

FURTHER EVIDENCE

Chapter Three discusses third parties. It also provides examples. Identify one of the chapter's main points. What evidence does the author provide to support this point? The website at the link below also discusses third parties. Find a quote on this website that supports the main point you identified. Does the quote support an existing piece of evidence in the chapter? Or does it offer a new piece of evidence?

Third Parties in American History

mycorelibrary.com/modern-political-parties

CHAPTER FOUR

THE WORK OF POLITICAL PARTIES

US political parties operate at all levels of government. Some minor parties may be in only one or a few states. The Republican and Democratic Parties are in all 50 states. The major parties have committees at the national, state, and county levels. These groups coordinate their efforts to get their candidates elected. Party committee members are sometimes

Volunteers man the phone banks at the Iowa headquarters of Republican presidential candidate Ted Cruz in January 2016.

Party Membership

Most American voters identify themselves as a Democrat or a Republican. This does not mean they are members of either party. It usually means that they tend to vote for that party's candidates. To become a party member, a person must officially register with the party.

elected by party membership. Party leaders may also appoint them.

Selecting Candidates

Political parties work hard to get their candidates elected. They look for candidates who have the same political views as stated in the party platform. But party members may hold different views on some issues. Candidates' views might even conflict with the official platform.

The first step is to find the right candidate. The best way is to ask voters. The parties may conduct research to ask what voters want.

The election process begins with primary elections. In these state-by-state elections, voters choose a candidate from their party to run in the

IMMIGRANTS VOTE!

Arab-American volunteers in Brooklyn, New York, check voter registration sheets before going door to door to urge voters to cast their ballots on Election Day in 2014.

general election. In some states, however, voters pick a candidate during a caucus. A caucus is a meeting of party members.

Parties choose their presidential candidate at a national convention every four years. The party wants a popular candidate. It usually picks the candidate who performed best in the primaries and caucuses. The party also presents its platform at the convention.

On the Campaign Trail

Parties support candidates as they campaign. The parties organize speeches, rallies, and debates. They also try to influence voters directly. They host voter registration drives. They

Vice President Joe Biden and President Barack Obama wave to delegates at the Democratic National Convention in 2012.

Candidates' signs line the sidewalk outside of a polling place in Illinois.

encourage people to vote on Election Day. Political parties also spend money on advertising. Some ads may endorse a particular candidate. Others attack the opposing candidates. These are known as negative advertising.

Political campaigns cost money. A national political party collects donations. The party then distributes the money to campaigns.

After an Election

Political parties also play important roles after elections. They help elected members work together. The out-of-power party plays an important role too. It may criticize elected politicians. It may offer different ideas or proposals. It will present its own candidate at the next election. In this way, political parties keep people talking about important issues.

EXPLORE ONLINE

Chapter Four discusses the role that political parties play in supporting candidates. A party tries to convince voters that its candidate is the best. The website below shows examples of campaign materials. What do these campaign materials have in common? How do they use symbols, colors, and words to influence voters?

2016 Presidential Campaign
mycorelibrary.com/modern-political-parties

POLITICAL PARTIES IN GOVERNMENT

P olitical parties play a key role in government. Party membership determines who gets on committees. These committees do much of the work in Congress. Every bill submitted to Congress is referred to a committee. The committee studies the bill. It decides whether it should become law. More Democrats in office means more Democrats

US Senator Dianne Feinstein led the Senate Committee on Intelligence from 2009 to 2015.

in the committees. The same happens when Republicans have the majority in office. In this way, parties have power over which bills are discussed.

Party Leadership

Each house of Congress elects a leader. The Speaker of the House is the leader of the House of Representatives. The Senate leader is called the Majority Leader. Each party also has an officer called a whip. The whip helps plan and carry out party strategy. His or her job is to try to convince party members to vote with the political party.

Speaker of the House Paul Ryan

Political parties also make decisions about bills. They form a party caucus, a conference of party members in Congress. Members within the party may disagree about an issue. The caucus works to find compromise. This helps the party function as a team.

Political Parties Today

Political parties have existed since the early United States. The earliest parties have faded into history. Others have changed their names or their focus. Today, the Democratic Party and Republican Party dominate the political landscape. Third parties continue to seek broader support. In the meantime, the two-party system remains a central part of American politics.

Extremists in Political Parties

Some Americans worry about elected officials with extreme views. Such people are often called political extremists. Extremists may be unwilling to compromise. They are sometimes blamed for a lack of action in the US Congress.

A man displays campaign stickers for 2016 Republican presidential candidate Senator Ted Cruz and Democratic candidate Bernie Sanders.

- There is no mention of political parties in the US Constitution.
- Some of the country's founders did not support the idea of political parties.
- The Republican Party and the Democratic Party are the two main political parties in the United States.
- The present-day Democratic Party is the country's largest political party.
- The first Democratic president was Andrew Jackson.
- The first Republican president was Abraham Lincoln.
- The Republican Party believes in a more limited role for government than the Democrats do.
- Any party other than the Democratic or Republican Party is called a third party.
- The three largest third parties in the United States today are the Libertarian Party, the Green Party, and the Constitution Party.
- No third-party candidate has ever won the presidency.

- The US system uses a winner-take-all system, in which the top vote-getter is the only one who is elected to office.
- Political parties hold primary elections before a general election to help choose their candidates.
- The Republican Party and the Democratic Party both hold national conventions to choose candidates for president and vice president. At these national conventions, the parties also publish their platforms.

Take a Stand

Political parties will likely continue to play a major role in presidential elections for many years to come. Do you think the country's two-party system is a good system? Do you think the country should do more to encourage third-party participation in elections? Why or why not?

Say What?

Studying history and politics can mean learning new vocabulary. Find five words in this book that you have never seen or heard before. Use the glossary or a dictionary to find out what they mean. Then write each meaning in your own words and use each word in a sentence.

Dig Deeper

After reading this book, what questions do you still have about political parties? Write down one or two questions to research. With an adult's help, find a few reliable sources that can help you answer your questions. Write a paragraph about what you learned.

Tell the Tale

Chapter Five of this book discusses how the parties decide their platforms. Imagine you are the leader of a new party. What will you make sure to have on your platform? Write 200 words about your policy and why it is needed. Be sure to set the scene, develop a sequence of events, and offer a conclusion.

GLOSSARY

ballot
a piece of paper used to cast a vote

democracy
rule by the people

despotism
rule by a person or authority with complete power

election
the procedure by which voters choose to determine who will hold public office

extremist
a person whose beliefs and views go far beyond those of most people

independent
a person who does not identify him- or herself with any particular party

policy
a course of action promoted by a political party or other group

political party
a group of people that has come together to gain control of the government by winning elections

primary
an election held by the political party before the general election

two-party system
a system in which two major parties (such as the Republican and Democratic parties) hold the majority of the power

LEARN MORE

Books

Finne, Stephanie. *How Political Parties Work.*
   Minneapolis, MN: Abdo Publishing, 2015.

Jackson, Carolyn. *The Election Book: The People
   Pick a President.* New York: Scholastic, 2012.

Websites

To learn more about American Citizenship, visit
booklinks.abdopublishing.com. These links are
routinely monitored and updated to provide the most
current information available.

Visit **mycorelibrary.com** for free additional tools for
teachers and students.

INDEX

ABOUT THE AUTHOR

Lydia Bjornlund is a freelance writer and the author of more than two dozen books for children and adults. She lives in northern Virginia with her husband, two children, and two cats and loves everything to do with American history.